1976

This book may be kept

FOURTEEN DAYS

A fine will be charged for each day the boo

POEMS BY E. L. MAYO

The Diver

UNIVERSITY OF MINNESOTA PRESS, MINNEAPOLIS
LONDON · GEOFFREY CUMBERLEGE · OXFORD UNIVERSITY PRESS

TABLE OF CONTENTS

THE DIVER

The Diver 3

The Dance of the Feather 4

A Poem Is a Mirror 5

The Long Way 6

Concerning the Human Image 8

The Pool 9

Forty o'Clock 10

Art and Logic 11

Inventory 12

THE PATIENT ONES

The Patient Ones 15

The Free 16

Crusoe 17

Anglo-Saxon 18

Entry into Jerusalem 19

El Greco I 20

El Greco II 21

Lincoln 22

Belphage: A Biography 23

An Honest Magistrate 24

Sonnet for Redheads 25

The Positivists 26

Elegy for "Slim" 27

The Mole 28

FAREWELL TO THE WIND

Farewell to the Wind 31

Metamorphosis 33

No Ghost 34

The Angel 35

Iron Gate 36

The Questioners 37

Sonnet for the Season 39

Ode 40

The Oaks 41

The Phoenix and the Turtle 42

Sonnet 44

Starlight Patrol 45

In the Tunnel 46

Prelude and Fugue 47

The Shirt 49

In the Web 50

WAGON TRAIN

Wagon Train 53

1939 54

To Urizen 55

Sooth for the Chancellor (1939) 56

On the Student Peace Strikers Who Went to War . 57

I Had Seen Death Come Down 58

Transitional 59

New Hypothesis 60

The Uninfected 61

The Forgotten Soldier 62

In the Time of the Great Wind 63

They Say the World Was Weighed 64

The Signposts 65

To Catch the Common Face 66

THE DIVER

THE DIVER

Dressed in his clumsy, stiff, aquatic clothes,
His helmet screwed fast on so that he can
Do, say, see nothing in the world of man,
The diver shambles to the boatside, goes
Down the ladder, and the waters close
Over the steel that seals his sacred brain.
Over the boatside lean, his shadow scan
As it descends, shapeless and wavering.
It is no devilfish, is still a man—
But now it's gone.
           Creatures beyond our ken
He will describe in words on his return—
Pale words for objects seen—
The inhuman life that swirled before his sight,
Or fled, or fought. The treasure he seeks out
May yet be lifted up by creaking crane,
Splashing, out of the green, but in his brain
The jungles of the sea must flower still,
Whose hook has drawn the pale blood of the shark,
And when his streaming bulk climbs back aboard,
We'll mutter, say some contract has been signed
With what lies under, and that that occurred
Which has no human gesture and no word.

THE DANCE OF THE FEATHER

You have seen me do the dance of the dagger;
Next I shall perform the dance of the feather;
This is more difficult, yet easier, too.
In the first the blades are not supposed to touch you
But sometimes do; in the second you float around
As though held up by something invisible,
And sometimes the breeze lets you down,
But that is a part of the dance, an integral part:
Feathers don't fall like iron, of course,
But gradually, until everybody sees
It's drifting down at forty-five degrees
Or thereabouts, an inch above the floor,
And then some warm wind coming under a door
Finds the gray fluff and sends it up again—
Not far, not long—you never can be sure
Where it is going, what it's going to do—
That too is a part of the dance and half its charm.
Eventually of course it comes down,
Or at least I think it does—that isn't clear,
And sometimes halfway through I get a new idea.

A POEM IS A MIRROR

A poem is a mirror held to nature,
But it should be a magic mirror, showing
Clearer than to our shadowy sense, the glowing
And waning of a more than mortal creature,

And like calm stars above the anxious wind
Poems should allay with presentness our aching
For phantoms and their fashion of forsaking—
More tangible than earth, more real than mind.

THE LONG WAY

You always know, and knew
You have forever not to speak a word—
The groves there, stirred
By no hail, no wind.

You always choose, therefore,
The other, the long way—
The rocky ledge by the sea,
Hairy with sea-grass, glare
Sun without shadow. This

Is the best and the worst.
It does not last long:
The beach at once gives way
To the Concessions,

(The children, amphibians, expend
On water and on shore a summer's day,
But tanneries and mills where hides are cut
Is where their years are put),

Behind the canvas mountains, tenements:
Here, if you have a cent,
After pop, popcorn, lemonade,
You take the ferry, blunt at either end,
The common, general expedient.

Then the train takes your sunburned nausea
(A good day never dies)
With heat, with cinders, and with memories.

And subways squeal and turning turnstiles say
"Come, come away,
World-without-end-hurled, heavy, heavy eyes."

So—till the final owl-car's yellow glare
Extends to foot its stair
Elongating your bones to people in
Everett, Malden.

Oh be enough awake then if you can
To press bell for the cemetery stop
(Or plod five blocks if you go by that gate),

Then the short street where no house shows a light
And snoring is not heard,
Up the plank walk that bumps beneath your tread
And home, and never, never speak a word.

CONCERNING THE HUMAN IMAGE

Men who have seen
The human image in the Shakespearean glass
Distinguish Xerxes from Leonidas.

And though their mouths are stopped and shouted down
Hear more clear for that the hollow groan
Raised by the javelin of Laocoon.

And if they walk on pavements of no sun,
What's that to you at the world's ringside, releasing,
Bulletin by bulletin, the Dawn?

Sometimes renewed, but not by their own will
(Out of themselves only bad music still,
Shrill, grating, and—oh yes, you're right, afraid).

Yet they have seen the image Will descries
Shrug down Calvin's Hell, snap Cromwell's blade,
And grinning there at Marx in Paradise.

THE POOL

This is the pool that Plato visited
In the late Indian summer of his year
To eat the golden honey harvested
By his own bees in June and July sun.

The stench and smothering out of the wick of our time
Blackens, cracks, and dries
The calm Madonna with Leonardo's eyes;
The rock she sits among
Waits in a bombsight to be otherwise.
She sees the falling leaves and dying leaves
That cling there still, or looking through the brown
Woven horror of the boughs, she sees
The empty, arching skull.

But things above still find their counterparts
Under this water: tree responds to tree
And hill to hill; the smallest flake that flies,
Glassed in the pool, finds as it falls its own
Minutest properties.

The numbered angels of Pythagoras
Pressing upon us from the upper air,
Marrowless, cold—how should they speak us true?
But in the pool, ugly or beautiful,
All are compact of pity and of fear
As we are, only real.

FORTY O'CLOCK

It hardens, time hardens, the light,
The heart hardens. It is forty o'clock.

Poe's luminous forehead struggling in the gross
Bushes of memory
Bodily sensations of loss
Inability to tear off the burning
Garment of invisibility.

From lights in spring that tremble over water
Take endless trains in subways. Learn to know
The faces underground.
Where else shall love be found?
Or Hart Crane's face but where he once saw Poe?

The old man in the park feeding squirrels and pigeons
Is not by them regarded with suspicions.

O parks, night streets, dim shops, and then the door
Where children's eyes more beautiful than blue
Water without shadow
Shine and shine and shine and do not know.

Here where the world's variety grows narrow
The first fruit (or the last, if none should follow)
Is found in tangled grass, the puckering taste
Of getting used to slowly becoming a ghost.

ART AND LOGIC

Logic is a thing like steel rails,
Straight, with death at the end,
Or like Freud consigning Europe to the bow-wows
Unless the myth he forged from his own fate
Make Europe turn again.
But in non sequiturs like mummy wheat
Or green toads sealed in ancient concrete,
Art begins where contradictions meet.

INVENTORY

Now I have lain upon too many beds,
Intent, unsleeping, with wide-open eyes
Waiting a splitting open of the sky
That does not come. No easy symmetries
Could take me—agile life on anxious earth
Makes music bright as pewter in Dutch kitchens
Crumple, melt, and blacken in the heart.
Only what I could see from where I stood
I wrote about, and all I count good
Is no more than the leavings of a mouse
In a huge, dark, uninhabited house.

THE PATIENT ONES

THE PATIENT ONES

The patient ones, if they can keep a friend,
If they can love, if they can only sleep,
If they can only keep
Quiet, and with their brows
Furrow the air like prows
Toward whatever shipwreck waits them in a minute,
Shall squeeze out the last drop of meaning in it,
But they must keep as quiet as they can,
For words are dreadful to a quiet man
Except such speech
As courtesy may teach.
Thus, while they are in time, blind hopes will rise
To nourish them and all their days will pass
Quietly, waiting a hypothetical spring,
And while they foot it on
Under blank skies or over burning stone,
Like crickets in the Valley of Dry Bone
Sometimes they will sing.

THE FREE

The poor have houses that are wondrous gray,
Color of wind and rain,
Color of woodsmoke on October days
When the last leaves come down.

And they have hands and eyes
That touch nor see not what they dream upon,
And in their yards and in their houses lies
All rubbish that the world is tired of.

And so Necessity, the rag picker
Who has no liberal views,
Bargains beneath the clotheslines in their yards,
And they alone have power to pick and choose.

CRUSOE

Whenas from rocks the mist unblooms and clears
Crusoe awakes upon the strand, the shore
Where ships return no more.

His lifted eyes discovering no trees,
He thinks how many days, how many years
Piercing as nails shall mortify him here.

Accept, O Lord, this bottle of his tears.

The supernatural rigor of this land
Is nullified by neither curse nor song;
Nor can the greenest parrot's loudest squawk
Shelter the mind from the eternal rock
And bones of creatures gnawed and thrown away.

And it is tongueless being castaway.

And while his dusty head turns gray, burns brown,
He will think wistfully how sailors drown,
And being time's deepest scholar, study well
Every unwatered word beneath the mind,
And he will write it down
That after after there is after still.

ANGLO-SAXON

King Alfred sensed among his country's words
England's destiny;
But Caedmon, rapt, among his master's herds,
Felt all their history:
How all men, once, had owned a common tongue
And clumsy dialects the wide world over
Remembered music that the first had sung,
And would discover,
Through cries confused, the excellent, true stem
And scattered vowels of Jerusalem.

ENTRY INTO JERUSALEM

Under the billows where their bowl went down
The Three Wise Men of Gotham rub their eyes
To see in coral to the watery skies
The towers of a most impossible town.

On pavements that their knowledge proved a fraud
They enter softly, hiding their disdain,
That shallow persons should succeed again
And anthozoans be the Sons of God.

EL GRECO I

See how the sun has somewhat not of light
Falling upon these men who stand so tall;
See how their eyes observe some inward sight
And how their living takes no room at all—
Their passing stirs no air, so thin they are—
Behind them see small houses with small doors;
The light comes from an unfamiliar star
That lights their walls and falls across their floors.
What shall we say when one of these men goes
Into his house and we no longer see
His eyes observing something that he knows?
And if their houses brim with radiancy
Why does no light come through as those doors close?

EL GRECO II

The Greek began where color ends, with black,
And wooed the spectrum from the heart of night,
And though sometimes he trembled and turned back,
Painted as near as mortals do to light.
He knew that pictures for the ages' wear
Are not by tender colors hatched and nursed,
Nor pay the reckoning of time and air
Unless they stood on darkness from the first.
The Greek began with things that make men grieve:
The heartbreak and the certainty of night,
But in the very midst could still believe
And on his canvas generated light
Like the great sun that on so black a thing
Maintains the tall, blue, catholic sky of spring.

LINCOLN

Something he trusted in us, and we fed
On his idea and held it in our mind;
His faith grew true through our love of him—dead;
And none dared touch the charged circle—his mankind.
But the machine was there and its demand:
What could we do but feed those jaws for pay
When there were no more prairies, no free land?
Yet, in the end, we thought, we'd go Abe's way,
Prove he was right—no need for any alarm—
And stay ourselves, though we were wheels to wheels
Whose steel teeth grate the rhythms of shop and farm
Down to an iron throb that never feels,
Or feels as useless friction, flesh and blood's
Parity and Lincoln's platitude.

BELPHAGE: A BIOGRAPHY

Belphage wrote well, and from the top of his mind
Reported incidents and appearances.
Profound, significant, charitable, resigned—
We thought he could not alter. Entrances
Were made in him by care in his fortieth year.
He wrote no more because he would not carve
Personal sorrow into prose. The fear
Grew up in us that even Belphage could starve.
Almost he did, but in the interval
He was a child for wonder; as his brain
Grew leaner he perceived as comical
The explanations comfortable men maintain,
Saw holding up the rational facade
Nothing but angels, laughed, believed in God.

AN HONEST MAGISTRATE

Picture of an honest magistrate
Sifting the wheat from the chaff of what they said
In the case of the vanishing Jew the night before
    Passover:

The stone on the tomb, it seems, weighed nearly a ton
And made enough noise as it fell to waken the dead.
The guard report it pitched them onto the ground
And they found the stone five feet from where it
    had stood.

A spiced napkin, supposed to have wrapped the head,
They found carefully folded, separate
From the other cerements.
                            Common robbery?
Mystification to confuse the scent?
Calmly to prepare for the event?

He seems to have risen alone
With time and to spare, but he must have had help with
    the stone.

SONNET FOR REDHEADS

Red hair is dangerous; it goes deep in,
Feeds at the central fire and so must burn,
And as men who work at ovens and furnaces turn
White, not red, your redhead has white skin.
And though the heat of the sun is crueler
To them than others, burns them, freckles them,
It cannot change their white to swart or dim
The holocaust reflected in their hair.

Nero and Socrates and Lancelot
Will witness this, and Antony's sharp queen,
England's eighth Henry, great Elizabeth,
Blake, Verlaine, Villon, and—take one more breath—
Shaw, Beatrice, Cesar Borgia, Magdalene,
Christ, William Shakespeare, and Iscariot.

THE POSITIVISTS

The old like brown leaves crisp and cling
To what on earth may nearest lie;
All things which the adventurous mind
Finds out turn doubtful by and by,

But what is here because it is,
Because sere fragile fingers feel
Against them this, the old men say
That this is wisdom and no lie.

But in the silence where they toast
Dry toes beside a failing fire
The young man frets within his ghost
And shines his shoes and combs his hair.

ELEGY FOR "SLIM"

He will mount Jacob's ladder saw in hand,
Sucked cigarette between oblivious lips—
Not mortal now—through cutting out despond
Eternal to his tar-stained fingertips.

Hands that cut off dead limbs to save live trees,
Eyes that perceived death's shapes in the Argonne,
Feet that with whiskey's aid for twenty years
Climbed elm trees through annihilation

Now at the very top of that tall tree
That shadows all the world, but bears the sun.

THE MOLE

When the mole goes digging
He never meets a soul;
The stars are inattentive
To the motions of the mole.

He digs his frantic tunnel
Through chalk and clay and slime
His never-ending tunnel
A mouthful at a time

Alone; no planet bothers
To tell him where to dig,
For moles are very little
And worlds are very big.

And when his tunnel ceases
The little mole lies stark,
And at his back is dimness,
And at his head, the dark.

So to the mole all honor
And the labors of the mole,
With doubtfulness for tunnel
And ignorance for goal.

FAREWELL TO THE WIND

FAREWELL TO THE WIND

It fell upon the street and shook the house
And shook it like a rat, in pure fun.
I knew it was for me the wind had come.

We met beside a river. The night was dark
Save for one light on the other side of the water
That tangled with the water
When the wind flung upwards the plunging branches
   of trees.

I did not speak but sat on a bench by the river
And smelled the Red River
And autumn in August, and I watched the trees
Giving themselves whole to the wind's will.

(But mine was not the wind's, and moved in me
As when a man in a strange country
Encounters, not a friend, but the child of a friend.)

Then the wind spoke to me
Flinging a great arm across my shoulder,
Saying: You seem older;
Yet you are Mayo still, and I am he
Who shook a door once till you woke and came,
And we climbed to the top of Waite's Mount in a
   thunderstorm
And wrestled together in the roaring rain.

And after the long heat of the Bahamas
When your shoes were tight and your mouth confirming
   death
I slammed back the shutters of the dining room,
Chairs over tables, dishes over the floor,

With a puff of my breath,
And we walked all night together along the shore.
Sand stung your cheeks, and foam,
And my voice rose like an organ in the cathedral
Of human life, blowing the chorale
Of victory in the teeth of the world's pain.
Now we are met again.

What could I do? Hunched on the bench by the river
With his hand on my shoulder
Whose laughter lives forever?

Wind—I said—
Breaker of ties, breaker of promises,
Glad would I let your grasshoppers attend
The weedy garden of my daily bread,

But I have chosen of late
This people for my people
And their fate is my fate.

You are the shaker of the earth's four corners
And winnow them one by one,
But you cannot shake or winnow the four corners
Of my stone heart, and in those cluttered corners
Humbly, by accident, my work is done.

His arm leaped from my shoulder. He was gone,
Yet paused at the bend where the trestle crosses the
    river
To cry out thrice for scorn upon my end—
I had known that this was the way it would end
That first night on the hillside in the storm
But not that one day I should look upon
This wanderer as the beautiful child of a friend.

METAMORPHOSIS

My shadow strides ahead and towers before me.
It is a most portentous-looking shade.
Is this the man my mother thought to have made
Before the truth came squalling and she bore me?
Look closely: Does it wear a coat of brown?
And brown shoes? spectacles? and need a shave?
Then it is surely me. I think we have
Changed places under this El Greco moon.
I am my shadow now and he the man,
And being chained to him I have to trot
After those heavy steps that tramp and tramp—
Now shrinking up, a pygmy African,
Now Gulliver, the slave of Lilliput;
But I'll be night when he puts out the lamp.

NO GHOST

There is no ghost climbing by wavering lines
To aid you; under earth there is no eye
Follows you; at your birth
Only Death, your Death that knows this house,
Took thought for you, stood ready to assist
Delivery from all your mother bore,
Nor held, nor hurried you, as if to say:
"Will and take your fill and then I may,
For what is flesh itself but my door?"

THE ANGEL

Eden was every man to me
Before my eyes had learned to see,
But when I sought their secret place
I met an angel face to face—
An angel with a flaming sword
In each man's soul stood up on guard,
To fend me off both night and day
And fend my burning love away.
I did not know the angel's name
In days when my young heart took flame,
But now I know it—or can guess—
The angel's name was Loneliness.
I love her better than I did
For now she keeps my secret hid,
And if she kept me out before
Now she keeps others from my door.
The broken shoes of indolence,
The mantle of deceit, the sense
Of soft threads weaving day by day
A certain web a certain way—
These are my own; no man may see
The unspeakable and secret me.

IRON GATE

To pass the thirtieth year is but to be
Other than one expected, barer here
The heart is than it was in many a year,
No longer cluttered with bright privacies.

Here Solomon perceives he is not wise
And with an eye upon the second prize
Divides desire with possibility;

Sometimes will talk with sailors of the sea
Because the sea gull in his proper breast
Beats louder now against a thinner door;

Lives now by miracle, and living tests,
In quiet desperation, by the clock,
The shifting shadows on the changeless rock,
But cannot guess what evening they portend.

He tries all things except the way to mend.

And since his certitude not always beams,
Snatches the shining runners as they fly—

Where nothing shall have nothing to repent
Even the awkward song is excellent—
And he has heard the thunder through his lie.

THE QUESTIONERS

The sad sage-gray Dakota hills
That stood around me at my mapping table
Pestered with flies stay with me; the great
    moaning
Of wind that walks that country day and night—
The years of famine and the years of blight
Are in that wind, and all the helpless anger
That men defrauded turn against themselves
Before they lift their rifles from their
    shelves.
And I have seen the ghosts of the Dakotahs,
Out of revenge on white men, smut the corn,
Ride like Russian thistles on the dust storm,
Crack earth with drouth, as hoppers darken
    the sun.
And I have heard the foxes on the hill
Barking a question; insects at the sill,
Drawn by my lamp, as they flung themselves at
    the flame,
Whirred with their wings no other name but
    my name.
I have stepped from farmhouse kitchens and
    been drowned
In the great empty of the country nights
And seen the Northern Lights
Beam after beam shoot over, seeking me.
But I would not be found, and would not cry
"Here! Here am I! Send me!"

Or whisper from the ground,
For I knew I could not answer such hard
    questions
And better never heard and never found.
And yet I never cease to ponder the questions
Of the creatures of the country without trees,
But all the answers I know are wordy or bloody,
Sick with swords or social disease;
And though my country silence answered nothing
And vigilance and patience are unsure
I have given my love to the askers of hard
    questions
Till what discovers darkness finds dark's cure.

SONNET FOR THE SEASON

The erstwhile rich green earth growing barer now
And bushes all transparent; I can see
Precious little left for you and me
In fields where promise withered row on row;
And that is why details leap forth and stun,
Though there before; the foliage being gone,
Right through the ribs of that vast skeleton,
Once all the world, we see this different one.

Come! Through the ribs with you! Already here,
I sniff the funny air, groping your hand;
And I can see a thing from where I stand
Who can believe in six months of the year?
Yet here it is, and on my coatsleeve, too:
The first precise unerring flake of snow.

ODE

O early launched by terror into terror
To be in her gray eye a lonely runner,
Look in your own heart for her last answer:
"I," she replies,
"Am your own compromise."

One clean window were enough sky
To stand upright in but for compromise,
This evening in things, sifting
Into the brain like sleep, smoothing
Contrition and anger
Till they are only slumber
Under the sun and bones under a hide.

O Eye propped in the shade
To see the race the lonely runner made,
Caryatid, cajoler of days,
Foster nurse, beguiler of all sense,
Precise in consequence,
Double, and twin, Nature, receive man's praise.

THE OAKS

All we know is there
And all we cannot know because the mind
Is shaped to no such knowledge, and I turn
Homeward at evening from my quarries there
To see you sitting by the window, or
Facing the windless trees through the glass in the door.
I cannot speak
Of these things any more, cannot say,
See, they are gone; this is a holiday.
But one will turn a page and there will be
Scrub-oak branches twisted every way
And turn another, wondering to see
The same branches under the same sky.

The strong laboring wings of birds
Return through the still air
And it is spring so far as spring occurs
Where these oak trees are.
Who would have guessed that only we, we two
Should ever know these oak trees through and through?
Or know the true, secret name of the river
That curls beyond them through brown mist or blue?
Or that tall tower on the other side of the river
With one small window and no visible door?

THE PHOENIX AND THE TURTLE

Supposing all imaginable good
Accessible, and our living eyes could see
Unscalpeled of the gray prenatal film,
Where should we find it, think you, here at home?
Maeterlinck's bluebird by the kitchen sink?
Or boding in the light of summer sky
Apocalyptic with the thunderstorm?
Surely some sigh that rises and departs
Departs toward this? Some sensitive pulse in your wrist
Throbs faith at mention of felicity?
But when you hold the delicate fluttering creature
Dissonance comes, and the thing you held in your hand
Fades like the last cry that the winds take over
From some lost swimmer swallowed from the eye
In the gray, sucking sea's deformity.
Felicity is not for you and me;
And saying this with quiet level eyes
Calm on each other's faces, we shall be
Living creatures moving through the dusk
Distinguishing the seagull from the sea.
And we shall view the world with accurate eyes:
The sparrow's small voice quickened by the rain,
The contemplation in the mourning dove's
Four level tones will speak more nearly to us.
And what shall be whatever we do or say
We shall not know, nor know the imaged sky
We people with dying memories of the dead,
But confident in knowledge of the black
Rough rocks of this world, we shall keep our eyes
Intent on actual landscapes while we keep

Our scrupulous hunger polished like a sword
Until we flesh it in the thing adored;
For Euclid lied, and in this crooked world's
Cruel political geometry
Only the accurate eye,
Agile, intent, patient in one desire,
Shall see, perched high upon a telegraph wire,
The Phoenix and the Turtle of content.

SONNET

On the warm air the breathing branches keep
Company with sunlight through the leaves;
On the white house next door the shadows sleep
Through the long afternoon, and June reprieves
The mind—that ancient malcontent—from thought
Of what must be, of that harsh bugle horn
That cries of one more battle to be fought,
Friend from friend parted, lover from lover torn.
Myra, there sounds the horn, and my indenture
Was of my own hand's signing. I must go
Under this dappled light on new adventure;
None but ourselves shall guess or ever know
That in such parting only shadows part—
Leaf-shadows on the homestead of the heart.

STARLIGHT PATROL

Eyeshine of God, the scorn of stars wears down
Impertinences of time, and we regard
Through nets of blood, the nerves' interstices,
Steel starlight piercing down.

Still, still on earth, the blood's dark river roars
Between us and our consummation;
There on the other bank, up there, so plain
They hurt like wounds, our treasure, love, and friend.

The end is mystery; until the end
Watch the windows blink out one by one,
The buildings harden, and the stars define
The harmless sleeping lineaments of Cain.

IN THE TUNNEL

I knew I should be here
Oh long ago,
Saw myself sitting here, scribbling here
Ten years ago,
But when I get up and leave this tunnel
I do not know where I shall go.

Thunder, spark,
Whistle cleaving the night
Glittering procession of light;
Then doubly
Dark.

Without the occasional sound
Of wheels going round,
Of trains going through,
Whistle and bell,
I should not know where we were
I should not know
I should sleep too well.

But here by sad commuters compassed round,
In the long tunnel
In blown, foul air, awaiting the quickening sound
Of wheels going round, I have seen
Soiled paper, torn
Newspaper softly blown
Down the long tunnel, I have known
The vision of crumpled paper and cannot get home.

PRELUDE AND FUGUE

Ascending alone at birth between the great
And lesser lights, the planets being placed
According to plan,
To earth I came, on earth my body was
Delivered weeping; I had left my sword
In safe hands somewhere behind Aldebaran;
But coming alone like this
Without insignia to tell the man
I could not guess my lineage or name,
Despaired of vindication, set my mind
To quarry up the only hard stone
Here in the Middle Kingdom—
Harder than that of Michaelangelo's *Night*—
Called Time, and out of this to build my tomb,

My tomb and house to last, because no bomb
Could shatter work of the least artisan
In this tough medium.

II

You see the shaky scaffolding, the stuff,
The often halted gougings, all the blocked
Ugly first motions—sometimes see me hurl
My hammer in the corner and go out
To take the measure of the meaningless night—
And doubt me; and I doubt,
                          but coming back
I always see this fingerpost or sign,

See it without a light when nights are dark,
Upon it, THOSE ARE PEARLS THAT WERE HIS EYES:
And all I know and take for world and wise
Puts on a certain incongruity,
Rises at midnight through the face of the clock
Or on my way to work
Like sunlight on the faces of the slain
Moves like laughter, and the task is plain:

No peace for you or me or any man
But labor with hard stone in all between
The laying down behind Aldebaran
Of his good sword and taking it again.

THE SHIRT

Silence more deep than silence is before
The whistle of the midnight local; deeper
Closer and colder than the element
That is to darkest swimmers palpable,
Such silence; and such winds as ever blow
Down certain forked abysses have conspired
To weave for me the garment I wear now,
The shining shirt I dreamed of and desired.
The mind that stood aghast
The heart that beat so fast
To see what it had seen
Are fitted out at last;
I had not thought the universal tailor
Had such an eye, could make a fit so clean.
This is the shirt that the most pitiless storm
Could not prevent from keeping a man warm.
And none dare steal it—none!
Even the raggedest beggar would not plunder
This splendid shirt, though he should freeze to the bone.
Moreover, it is known.
Only the other day a man I know
Remarked upon it, found it food for wonder
That Hercules wore a very similar number
A number of years ago.

IN THE WEB

What you desire not starlight nor tearose
Breathing at evening from the bush by the house
Tells, nor does the dialect of water
Hissing from the faucet or the hose
Gossip of your loss.

They keep your secret well until you die,
And as the colors of the evening sky
Burn to darkness down, each solemn color
That blesses you before it turns its shoulder
Is tacit with your ghost.

Huge as the night with stars above your house
These patterns laid on emptiness revolve
Beyond all searching; seeds you scatter strive,
Determined things, beyond the studious
Solicitudes of love.

This night and every night they dance in fire,
These patterns of the slayer and the slain,
And now a cock with half his feathers gone
Crows for a dawn he shall not see again
And cannot but desire.

WAGON TRAIN

WAGON TRAIN

As pioneering children, when no rain
Made water brackish in the last canteen,
Went right to sleep, and just as seldom knew
When guns were cocked and ready all night through,
So do we ride the earth's revolving wheel,
Moving across what prairies, to what wars,
Against what ambush, eye does not reveal;
Nor do we know what loyal outriders
Swing on to clear our path across the plain,
But drift to sleep where canvas hides the stars
Of the long planetary wagon train.

1939

Tell me, daemon eyes that know
All that grows invisibly
About us, what it is that you
See that our eyes cannot see.

I see the vegetable years
The thicket in the thinking mist
Drip incredible black tears
Over an old romanticist,

See the great trees that tempered noon
Thicken and lean about a house
Where no dog barks and no light shows
Through the gross trunks and twisted boughs,

And hear a whimpering within
Granted permission . . . then the sound
Of grinding key and lifting chain

And now the baying of the hound.

TO URIZEN

Take off, take off that burning crown
Of moon and stars, O Urizen:
The burden and the mystery
Take off and lay all down.

Your reign is done: the smallest hand
Groping for touch in blacked-out street
Twitches the circlet terrible,
The neon robe falls at your feet.

There will be no more progresses,
No lords to let you in,
But cindered earth where your feet go
And blood where they have been.

You will be hunted from sea and air
Rooted from earth till the kingdom
Of mere bare animal alone
The wide world over, come.

And animals shall rise and cry,
"We humbled Urizen."
But Los shall take your one good eye
And so begin again.

SOOTH FOR THE CHANCELLOR
(1939)

You who feel the texture of this time
By touch direct—and shiver,
Having seen certain horses eat each other
And one dead friend return,
Whether in company or solitude,
Be waiting for the one impossible sign,
Be waiting for the coming of the wood:
When the trees march, poor soldier, we shall see
Whether the cold that halters you at core
Will tighten as you struggle in that dawn
With the fighter who was not of woman born.

ON THE STUDENT PEACE STRIKERS
WHO WENT TO WAR

They said they would not go and then they did;
Into the violent. It was very fine,
But then, we did not know
Why they refused, in the first place, to go.
And what metallic thing
Ticks under their coats as they return
We have yet to learn.

I HAD SEEN DEATH COME DOWN

I had seen death come down like smoke at night
Or rise like mushrooms—this was nothing new,
Had been arranged beforehand, and I grew
Accustomed to its presence, viewed the sight
As in my native country, moved abroad
Inspecting collapsed buildings, leaning walls,
Condoling widows, and at funerals
Commending children to the unknown god.

Then came the death unlooked for: in the skies
Bright sunlight; on the faces, every one,
Smiles to the quick, the straight look in the eyes,
Much music, lest a man should think alone,
And at each bridge game and on every phone
Nothing but friendship, cheer, and enterprise.

TRANSITIONAL

Only between we live: nowhere;
And fair, high-hearted ones,
Who thought they would not stay here, stay here.
And our way outward from betwixt and between
Gets lost among the chimneys, through gray air
Rises columnar to the evening star
Eternal over incongruity.

O not by accident the paint turns gray
On these white houses or that money does
No more than everything for anyone—
In the amber of money lies beauty, the dead fly—
And none can check the scale of usury
That forms on damask lip and honest eye
Or the blood feud fought out in every alley
Of once upon a time with someday.

But since I shall not lust to say my say
Anywhere else or care what words mean,
Visit me, hard Muse, betwixt and between,
Armored well with pins of crooked fire,
To hook a remedy
Narrow as mother love, no heavier,
No stronger than the air,
And hands too deep for credible find me.

NEW HYPOTHESIS

For the vast quietness between the stars
The ugly tables and the rickety chairs
Comfort us; and till the universe
Yawns in its sleep, and lo! we are no more
We shall explore—
Opening and closing yet the soft pine door—
The mystery of better and of worse.
We should expect no better, we suppose:
Slapped cheeks, the giggled laugh, the throes
Of after liquor teach us to expect
Hard laughter, the shrugged shoulder, neglect
In age; yet hungry, crooked, or remiss,
The knowledge of the new hypothesis,
Cool in the stars, burns in our forehead bones:
That human life might be better than this.

THE UNINFECTED

I saw a man whose face was white as snow
Come slowly down the mall,
And he was followed by another one
Till there were seven in all.

Now this is very strange that lepers be
Allowed to walk abroad in broad daylight.
I shook myself, and quickly turned to call
A bluecoat, and as suddenly caught sight

Of one in blue ruling the thoroughfare
Who made me passage through that brawling sea
With one raised hand. I spoke, and he inclined
To hear my word, the face of leprosy.

I turned and went straight on to search my own
Face in the next shop window mirror-glass—
Still no infection, not a single spot,
So I stood there and watched the lepers pass

Till four drove up to take me to a place
Where I live now, attended very well
By several strong male lepers dressed in white,
Eating what I like, sound as a bell.

THE FORGOTTEN SOLDIER

We too, it seems, possess
The wit to send the cylinders of war—
Enjoying to a man
The delicate partnership of hand and gun
To wing the rare and wary bird of peace.

Oh not for us the time
Of fiddles playing over in the pavilion:
We stood outside like gray
Wolves in the moon, then bedded for a dime
Or rode the rails into the West's vermilion.

Many a morning in gray waking streets
We learned what clubs were for,
And learned the use of stockings filled with lead
And have been left for dead—
In many an alley learned this art of war.

We have been students almost everywhere
Since hunger taught us wit.
We know war to the bone—
But of a peace that follows after it
We do not know and have not ever known.

IN THE TIME OF THE GREAT WIND

Tonight the wind blows as it would blow down
The last tree, the last house, the last man;
Tonight the Allies leave Norway writhing
Like a cut worm under a boot stamped down.

All night planes in their scores keep laboring
From the new airport half a mile away,
And my heart labors with them, and the wind
Keeps blowing, blowing; this is the second day.

Now all the world grows insubstantial;
Only the wind exists, and it is steel
Scraping the world, and all not rooted well
Follows like old newspaper, comes to heel.

What will remain when it has blown its fill?
Not bread, not wine, not children's sticky hands,
Nothing, unless the hapless heart can wring
From wind, on wind, through wind its wayfaring.

THEY SAY THE WORLD WAS WEIGHED

They say the world was weighed
In golden scales a very long time ago
And tipped the beam; but now it is not so.
The fire is falling on America
And everything there is is straw, will burn.

Hurry, if you're only going through,
But if you stay, the thing is your concern.
No tea is in the harbor now, the tower
Shows not one light, nor two;
After this hour the fiery minister
And "Yes, sir! Yes, sir! Yes, sir! Certainly, sir!"

THE SIGNPOSTS

Airplanes will move across the raindark sky
    With healing in their wings;
Water will cool men's tongues when we shall lie
    Unknowing of these things.

Where we went wrong and could not find our way
    Back to the fork in the road
Signposts like pointing men will rise to say:
    "This highway is no good.

"Here travelers are changed; here they become
    Pillars of salt and stone.
Their minerals cry, 'Turn back, oh daughter, son;
    Take the appointed one!' "

TO CATCH THE COMMON FACE

To catch the common face which is all faces
The man whose name is Alpha and Omega
Calmly, as is his custom, paints the square,
The bombers zooming down, the thermit's roar,
The popcorn stand split open, the common face
As it was in the beginning and shall be—

Also, a quieter subject: boy with harmonica
Beside a girl in her mother's high-heeled shoes:
Their piping play, their growing pains, their mating—
Limns and gives each excellence its dues
Though these be all ignored in the every paper
And the boy's end be gas, the girl's the stews.

Day after day, among harmonicas,
Kisses, high heels, and money in munitions,
He circumvents the enemy's positions
And in this bloodstained, whistling shaft of stars
Follows the rare art as best he can
To catch the beautiful lineaments of man.